In Memory of Millie
May she be remembered with pride
and her soul rest in peace.

Introduction

Thank you for buying this book, the money raised will pay for the printing costs and the remainder will go to CRMI to support the work they do. This is actually the second edition of this book and although the first run only comprised of two books this allowed me to see what it would actually look like and for people to make comments about the contents, which after some thought I have incorporated in this edition. Some commented that they wish there had been some text underneath the photographs. The reasons for my decision are twofold: I believe a photograph in itself should tell a story and it was my hope and intention for the reader to contact CRMI or me so that they may learn more about the photograph and what the charity does. However, I have added additional comments to some of the introductions to the chapters.

In January 2018 I travelled from the UK to Uganda as part of a group who spent two weeks carrying out a medical mission on behalf of Christian Restoration Ministries International (CRMI) in an area north of Kampala. CRMI Children of Hope "whose aim is to find sponsors in the west for orphaned and destitute children in Uganda and to provide them with an education, health care and vocational training."

The team comprised of 19 in total.

5 Doctors: Simon Kaye, Mike Wong, Nick Johnstone, Alison Johnstone and Paul Wadeson.

5 Nurses: Sarah Melling, Sarah Gorst, Kathy Haughton, Meg Disberry and Marilyn Midgley.

1 Physiotherapist's assistant: Ehud Nir.

They were supported directly by a team of 6 people from the UK and 2 Ugandans. These were Juliet Burd, Margaret Calvert, Ruth Riley, Peter Gregson, Pauline Kaye and myself from the UK. The Ugandan's were Joel our driver and Ibrah Jo, who was the 'I can get anything and translate as well' man! There were also many Ugandans who interpreted, cooked, prayed and carried out all sorts of tasks, without whose help and support the mission would not have been possible.

During the two weeks 'Outreach' clinics were held for the communities of Bombo (3 clinics), Nakaseke (2 clinics) and Ssanga (2 clinics). The aim was to see children, family members and guardians who needed medical support.

I like taking photographs and I had taken my camera and hoped to get a few shots! What actually happened was that I had the privilege and was honoured (over the two week period) to be given total access to all areas of the mission. I took over 2000 photographs! What impacted on me was that the people of the areas we visited were generous in the way they approached life.

Compared with those in the UK, they appeared to have absolutely nothing and were grateful for the smallest of things. They have the most interesting, beautiful faces and incredible smiles (when you can eventually get them to do so!). Initially, they were understandably cautious and reluctant when I walked around with my camera. However, over the two weeks as they got used to me walking around they began to approach me to ask for photographs. The children seemed really intrigued, which fascinated me until one of the team pointed out that it was quite likely that they had never seen their own faces as they don't have mirrors!

Within this book, apart from the beginning of each chapter I have decided not to use names or descriptions. I wanted the images (particularly the faces) to tell their own stories. Obviously, it was a very difficult task to whittle down the number of shots to include in the book so that the end result wasn't the size of the full Oxford English Dictionary! In the end I tried to just scratch the surface and show a small reflection of those I saw and the wonderful team I was part of.

This book is meant not only as a tribute to all those involved in CRMI Uganda & CRMI UK. It is a small way of saying thank you to all those who allowed me to photograph them and to the hundreds in the UK who have supported the efforts of CRMI and have not been able or fortunate to go to Uganda to see first-hand the wonderful work that goes on there. I would also like to thank those who were brave enough to make comments about the original book, which I found useful and have included in this edition.

I have many memories of the trip; some happy, some poignant, but, my ever lasting memory will be the smiles of the wonderful people we met as part of CRMI and in the villages, towns and Kampala. I hope that I have been able to convey this within the pages that follow.

For those of a technical nature I used a Canon 7D MkII camera with a 'Tamron' 17 to 270mm lens. For the most part I used a program setting.

Finally.... If you are interested in the work of CRMI, want to support or sponsor a child or family please look at their website:

http://childrenofhope.org.uk

Tony Disberry
May 2018

The Children

Over the two week period in Uganda we saw a vast number of children in the clinics and in the countryside. I photographed hundreds of them. The one thing that struck me was generally they appeared to have nothing but they had the most wonderful smiles. To have to choose a handful of photos for this book was an unenviable task! There is no particular order in the choice that I finally made, the photographs just seem to fit!

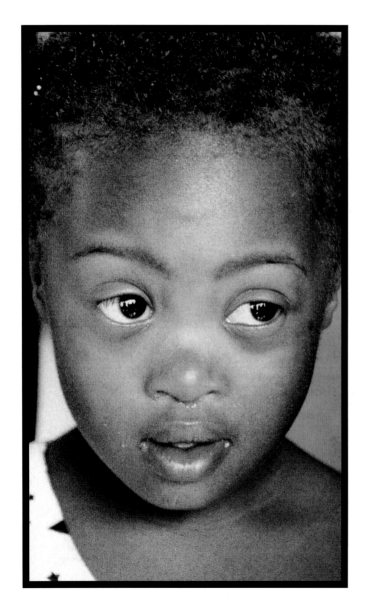

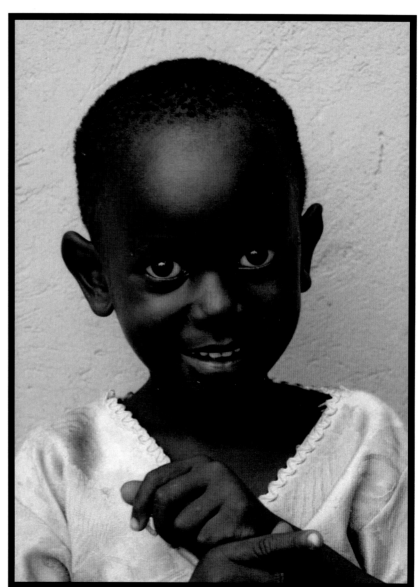

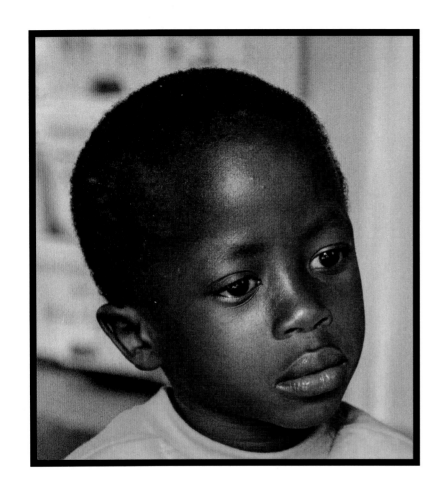

The Bore Hole

After a lot of thought, I have decided to include some photographs of a bore hole. Bore holes can be seen in a variety of shapes and sizes but the photos opposite are typical.

For thousands of Ugandans living in rural areas this is the only means of getting water. So the next time the tap plays up, or the water goes off for an hour or so think yourself lucky you don't have to walk miles carrying 5 Gallon containers!

The Clinics

The whole reason for the mission was to provide free medical care for as many people as practically possible. For those not familiar with how the clinics work the photographs may seem shocking. However, for those who received care and support it was often the only time they had ever seen a doctor and in some cases it was life changing and in one case actually a lifesaving experience!

Seven clinics were held in the two week period: Three at Bombo, (two initial clinics and a review/follow up clinic) and two at Nakaseke and two at Ssanga, (one initial and one review/follow up clinic at each place). These were held in the school at Bombo and the churches at Nakaseke and Ssanga.

As part of the clinics there were small educational groups that catered for children who had disabilities and female health and hygiene.

The pictures at the start of the chapter (which are outside) are what were used for waiting rooms at all three locations. The two photographs on the opposite page to the waiting rooms are the actual clinics at Nakaseke and Ssanga. There are photographs of the Bombo clinic as you look through the chapter. My aim was to give an idea of the conditions that we had to work in.

29

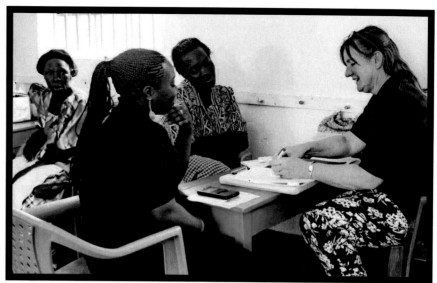

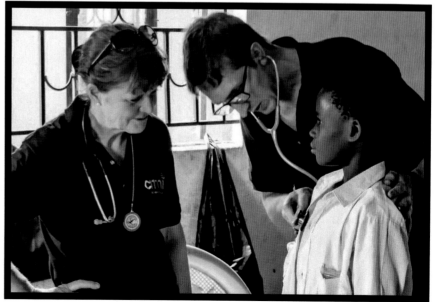

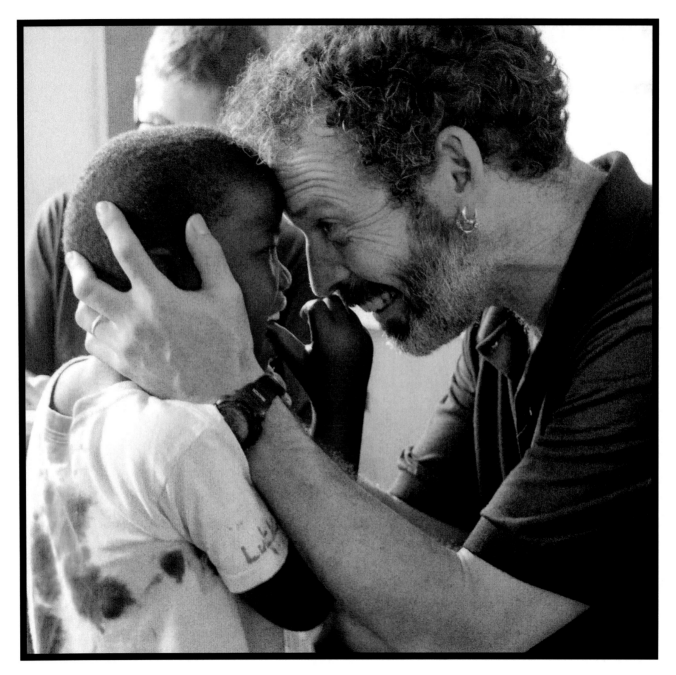

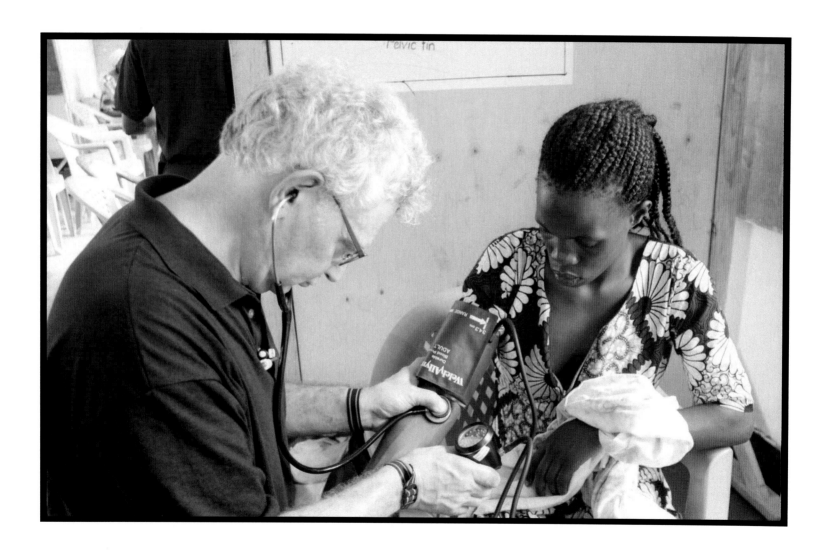

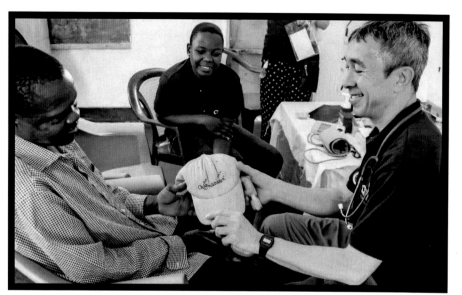

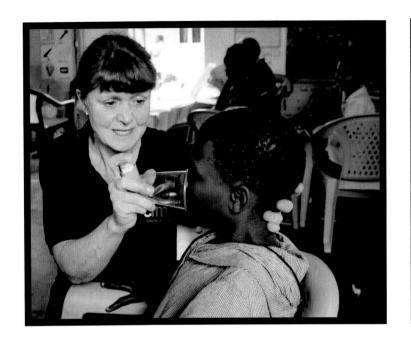
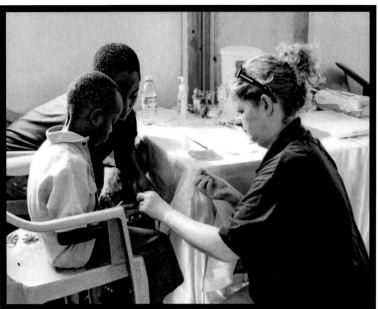

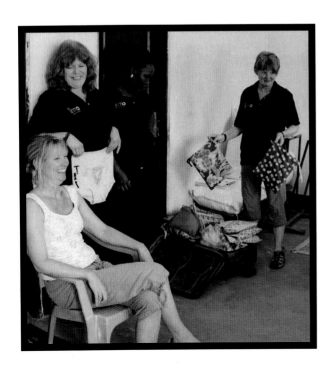

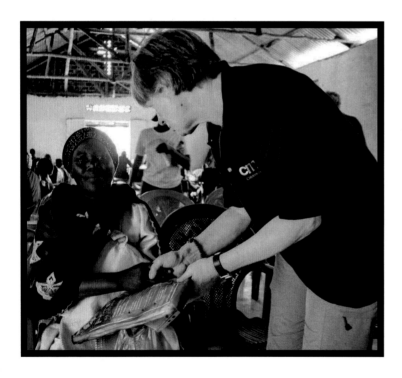

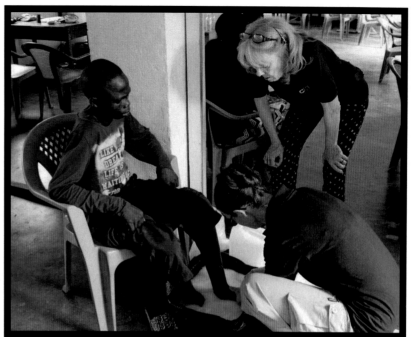

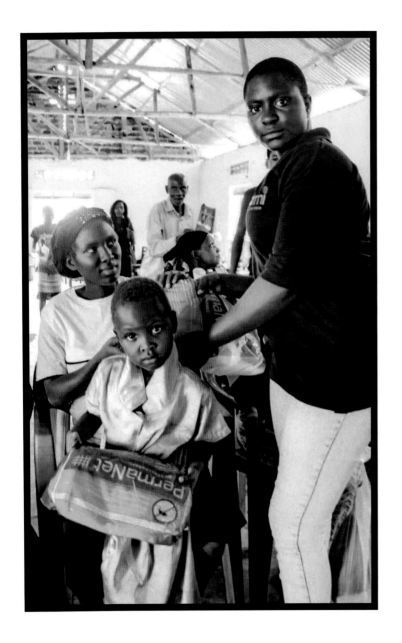

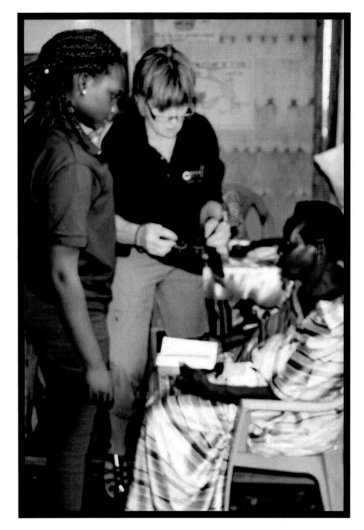

The Ugandan Team

Without the support of many Ugandans the medical mission would not have happened. There were many of them and they supported in a variety of different ways including interpreting, providing prayer support, cooking lunches, supplying everyday things that had not been taken out with the team and generally provided support when things got difficult.

Smiles

When one thinks about what power is? A smile is probably the last thing that comes to mind. However, the smile is one of the most powerful things a person has!

A smile can open conversations, open up hearts and even open doors.
A smile can heal people, solve problems and generally make people feel good.
A smile can and often does make the world a better place.

When we were in Uganda even though a lot of people appeared to have nothing by UK standards there were lots of smiles.

What you will see in the following chapter are a few of the smiles that I saw and I hope they bring a smile to your face too.

Disbo Photos

54

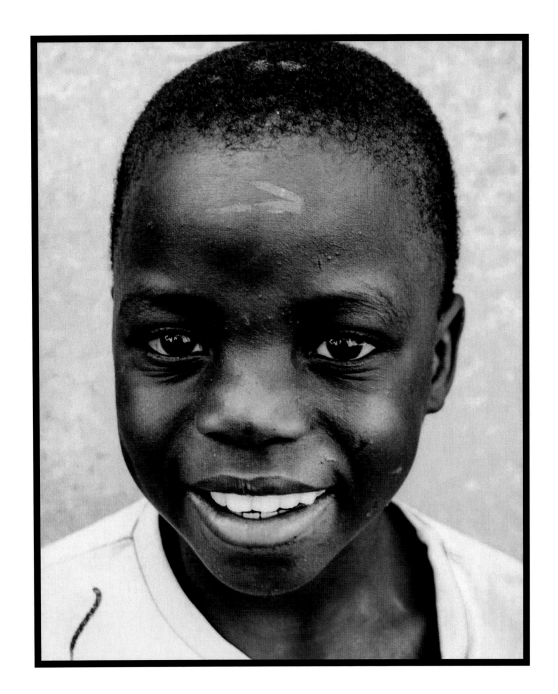

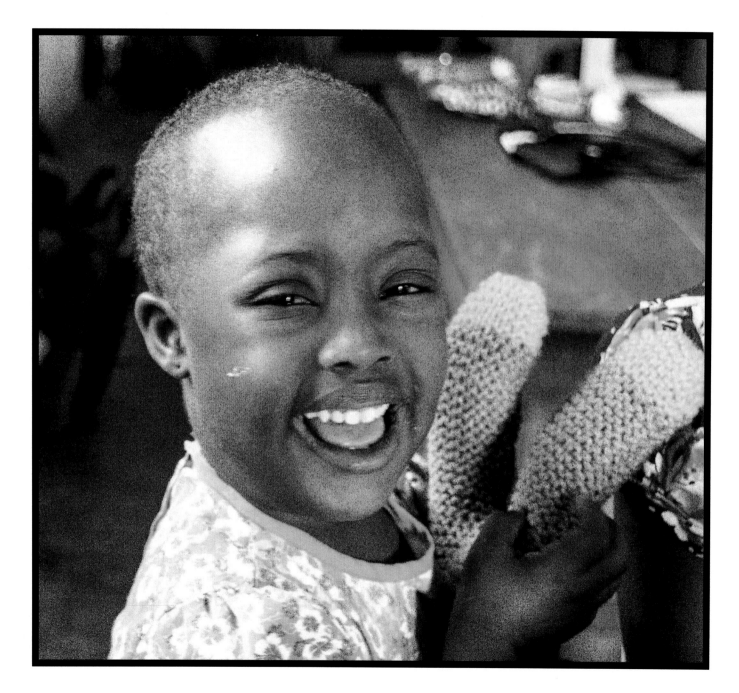

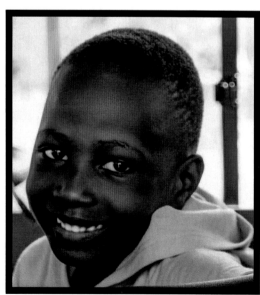